Six-Word Lessons on

EXCEPTIONAL CAREGIVING

100 Lessons to be a More Compassionate & Creative Caregiver

Mackenzie Daniek
BSN, RN, CHPCA, CHPN

Published by Pacelli Publishing
Bellevue, Washington

Six-Word Lessons on Exceptional Caregiving

All rights reserved. No part of this book may be reproduced or transmitted in any form or by any means, electronic or mechanical including photocopying, recording or by any information storage or retrieval system, without the written permission of the publisher, except where permitted by law.

Limit of Liability: While the author and the publisher have used their best efforts in preparing this book, they make no representation or warranties with respect to accuracy or completeness of the content of this book. The advice and strategies contained herein may not be suitable for your situation. Consult with a professional when appropriate.

Copyright © 2014, 2017 by Mackenzie Daniek

Published by Pacelli Publishing
9905 Lake Washington Blvd. NE, #D-103
Bellevue, Washington 98004
Pacellipublishing.com

Cover and interior design by Pacelli Publishing
Cover photo by Pixabay.com

ISBN-10: 1-933750-39-1
ISBN-13: 978-1-933750-39-2

Introduction

Ernest Hemingway was once challenged to write a book in six words or less. He wrote, "For sale: baby shoes. Never worn." Dr. Seuss was given a similar challenge to write a book using 25 words or less. The result of this challenge was *The Cat in the Hat*. I was very excited to be added to the talented authors of the Six-Word Lesson series and join the ranks of these amazing authors. In our "go go go" world where folks want quick, easy information, this felt like the perfect platform to give you some quick tips on caregiving that will make it easier without taking more of your valuable time. I have divided this book into 10 chapters based on questions I get in my classes, such as:

The differences between types of caregivers
Communication
Time management
Frustration with other healthcare professionals
What to do when it's time to go to the hospital
Bathing
Movement
Nutrition
Toileting
Self-Care

It is my sincerest hope that you will get some tricks, understanding and knowledge from these short lessons and that you will enjoy learning more about how to become an even more phenomenal caregiver.

Acknowledgements

My everlasting thanks will go to my most perfect husband, Nathaniel. I know you hate when I call you perfect, but I truly do not know how I am so lucky to have you. Every woman pleads for a man who is kind, caring, smart and does dishes. You are all this and pretty hot too.

My boys, Alex and Elisha, are so amazing. These two little men are incredible and I love your silliness and compassionate hearts.

My mothers, Terri and Betty, are the greatest inspiration a daughter could have. My moms are exactly what I wish all women were--strong, intelligent and compassionate. They both always encouraged their daughters to be strong women and caring ladies and these are such amazing gifts for a daughter to receive.

I also want to thank my oldest friend and my newest friend. Chris. It's crazy that it's been 22 years since we met in our humble trailer park days. I'm so glad we escaped together and found happiness in the Pacific Northwest. I am also so blessed by Katrina, who is without a doubt a gift directly from God. I was lonely and prayed for a friend who would "get" me and a week later, Katrina and I bonded over *Twilight*. My mood is immediately lifted by your kindness with every text and date to the movies.

Table of Contents

HCA, NA-C, Family. What's the Difference? 7

I Don't Know Where Time Goes 19

How Do I Care for Me? 31

Why Don't They do What's Needed? 43

When it's Time for the Hospital 55

Rub a Dub Dub: Shower Time 67

Up and At 'em: Time to Move 79

Food: is it Medicine or Poison? 89

Toileting: Number 1 and Number 2 101

What Did They Say? I Dunno 113

Six-Word Lessons on Exceptional Caregiving

HCA, NA-C, Family. What's the Difference?

… 1

Home is where the heart is.

Home care aides (HCAs) work in home-like environments. They are essential in keeping people with disabilities at home. Home care aides are quite excellent at meal planning, housekeeping, cooking and nursing skills such as bathing, grooming and feeding. Home care aides need to be trustworthy and caring, as they are left alone with the client for several hours.

Nothing like a good nursing assistant.

NA-C stands for nursing assistant-certified, (same as CNA). NA-Cs work in hospitals, skilled nursing facilities (for rehabilitation or extended stays) as well as home care settings. They are educated in vital signs, medical conditions, bodily functions, nutrition, infection control and many of the same things as home care aides.

Caring for family: the up side

Clients who don't feel good or who are struggling with disease or disability tend to do better with loved ones around. Loved ones "get" them and all their quirks and weirdness. When family members get involved, clients are able to stay at home longer. The client's stress tends to be lower, allowing for more quality of life.

Oh wait, there's another up side.

Because clients with family caregivers stay at home more often, clients get more benefits that come with staying at home. Studies show that clients who stay at home are happier and healthier and their disease processes are more stable. They need fewer hospitalizations and less medication. They eat better and move more. Depression is also greatly reduced.

5

Caring for family: the down side

Clients with family caregivers tend to be healthier, but there is a down side to being a family caregiver. We tend to treat family members differently than strangers. With family, we tend to be more resistive, negative and ornery. We tend to be kinder and more compliant around strangers. No, not everyone follows this tendency, but it is definitely something to consider.

How to decide. The right choice.

Deciding to be a family caregiver is a big choice. There are many factors to consider. What other obligations do you have? How many jobs are you carrying? Are your children grown or do they have special needs? How much help does your loved one need? Can you pop in and out or do they need constant care? Take all these things into consideration before you take on this role.

7

We want to be at home.

So you've decided on home care because that is where your loved one is most comfortable and healthiest. Who do you choose? The HCA or the NA-C? It depends on what kind of help your loved one needs. HCAs are better at companionship, emotional support, reminders and housework. NA-Cs are better trained to handle complicated medical concerns. If you need help, interview several people to pick the right one.

Which one is better for us?

HCAs are better trained to work with those who need medications. HCAs learn to assist with medications in their basic training. However, a registered nurse can delegate administration of meds to NA-Cs as well as HCAs, which is especially helpful for creams, drops, sprays and suppositories that clients can't do themselves.

9

What if a facility is better?

Home care facilities (like adult family homes and assisted living facilities) are definitely great options. Many provide excellent personal care, but they can also offer benefits that are hard to find in home care--activities, outings and companionship. Moving into residential living can be especially good for those who want more friendships and frequent programs to occupy their minds.

10

How can we all work together?

HCAs, NA-Cs and family caregivers can all work together to bring about the best quality of life for clients with illnesses or disabilities. HCAs and NA-Cs can easily provide respite care, nursing skills or intermittent care. Family members can provide emotional support, financial support and care at times when professional caregivers are not needed. It's all about collaboration.

Six-Word Lessons on Exceptional Caregiving

I Don't Know Where Time Goes

11

You must read *Take the Stairs*.

In the book, *Take the Stairs*, author Rory Vaden discusses how important it is to keep an extremely detailed calendar. Every single thing should go on your calendar. All appointments, family commitments, meals, exercise, even quiet time and meditation or prayer. Everything you want to do in a day should be organized in your calendar. Check out the book for help.

Prevail over the distractions. Start connecting.

Stop staring at screens. Sure, technology can help us organize our day and schedule, but it can also be extremely distracting. Texting, email, Facebook, Twitter, YouTube, games and TV can all eat up time that we should be spending with our client or family member. Set limits to your screen time so that it doesn't consume your calendar.

Selfishness at 5am. Get more done.

In the book, *Start*, by Jon Acuff, he discusses the idea of "being selfish at 5 a.m." He says that the things we want to do cannot take time away from important relationships like family or work. So do the "selfish" things you want to do at 5 a.m. Run, plan, meditate or enjoy quiet time at 5 a.m.

"Out of clutter, find simplicity" ~ Einstein

Using two lists is an effective way to manage your priorities. Take a piece of paper and fold it in half. One side will be a running to-do list of everything you want to do. The other side should be things that are most important to get done today. This will clear the clutter in your mind and your schedule.

Plan for the unexpected. It's expected.

Emergencies happen. Taking care of the ill and disabled means that unexpected emergencies will come up. So it's important to plan for them. Allow flexibility in your day so that when the unexpected comes up, you're able to handle it without all your other plans becoming a mess. Don't pack the day so tight that there is no flexibility.

16

Pharmacy is a caring busy business.

Put prescription refill dates on your calendar. Getting medications refilled is more complicated than simply making a call to the pharmacy. Sometimes insurance changes their formulary. Sometimes the FDA will disapprove a drug. Sometimes the manufacturer runs out of supply. Put refills on your calendar a week before they are due so there is time to deal with problems.

Perfectionism is a big fat lie.

Do not waste valuable time trying to be perfect. We are not perfect people. We do not care for perfect people. We do not operate within a perfect healthcare industry and we do not live in a perfect world. If you spend time and energy trying to make everything perfect, very little will get done. Let "good enough" be OK.

18

The best way to lose time

Multi-tasking does not actually save time. In fact it takes up more time. Your brain cannot physically do two things at once. Instead, when you are trying to multitask, your brain moves back and forth between tasks and you lose twenty-five percent of focus and efficiency every time this happens. Focus on one thing, get it done and then move on.

19

Don't spend time, invest in it.

Do the thing you hate the most first. Get it out of the way and out of your life. When this task is done first, it doesn't sit in the back of your brain taking up mental and emotional energy. You will be able to better focus and enjoy the other tasks you need to do.

20

You really can't do it alone.

Letting other people help you will not only free up time, but allow for better relationships. Let your client help with a few things. Encourage family and neighbors to help. This will increase dignity and independence. When your clients have a sense of self-worth, they function at a higher level. This makes care easier and decreases the client's distress.

Six-Word Lessons on Exceptional Caregiving

Six-Word Lessons on Exceptional Caregiving

How Do I Care for Me?

Self-care can be hard care.

Taking care of yourself is imperative to being a good caregiver. You can't care for other people if you don't care for yourself. Burnout leads to a cranky caregiver and cranky caregivers give poor care. They are not patient, kind, humble or creative. If you want to give the best care, you have to start by caring for you.

I just can't do it anymore.

When you come to a point in caregiving that you are annoyed instead of empathetic, you have what is known as "compassion fatigue." Compassion fatigue is a real problem because it's a big sign that you are headed to complete burnout. Burnout can lead to breakdown of relationships, health issues and poor caregiving.

No. No is a complete sentence.

There is power in the word "no." It can lead to better health, boundaries and relationships. Don't take on the world. You'll just end up letting someone down-- either you or someone you love. "No" doesn't have to be mean and can be a loving way to take care of yourself and in turn, someone else.

The dreaded E word. Embrace it.

Exercise has incalculable benefits. Thirty minutes of exercise every day is shown to elevate mood, reduce stress, reduce depression and anxiety, and increase positive thoughts. The benefits go on and on. It increases stamina and creative thinking. Problem solving becomes easier. You don't have to be a world class athlete, but you do need to include some exercise in your day to be an excellent caregiver.

Cliché? You are what you eat.

What you put into your body is imperative to your success as a caregiver. It's important to eat something green once in a while. Mint chocolate chip ice cream is delicious, but not really a healthy green option. Fruits and vegetables improve your mood, creativity and problem solving. They give you more energy and decrease your risk of infections.

Where's the good food? The treats?

Healthy food is important, but the occasional comfort food treat has great benefits too (relaxation, for example). It's important to enjoy the treats you love, but not use them to medicate frustration, anger or burnout. Have a piece of cake, pie or brownie as a way to connect to your client, but don't use comfort food to self-medicate.

27

"The greatest wealth is health." ~ Virgil

Don't ignore your spiritual health. Caregivers who have spiritual health have a sense of safety and security, more confidence and peace of mind. Religion is where a lot of folks get their spirituality, but not the only place. The key is to have an inner place to go to in order to clear your mind and seek answers.

28

Feed your mind. Feed your health.

Healthcare is an ever changing institution. By the time you have learned one skill, three others have newer, better procedures. According *The Household Physician*, written in 1905 by seven very educated physicians, carbolic acid was a safe and effective treatment for hemorrhoids. We know now that is neither safe nor effective. Keep learning. It is imperative to your health.

29

A good night's (or day's) sleep.

Sleep is important for physical and emotional health. The proper amount of sleep helps caregivers handle stress, solve more problems and manage day-to-day routines. The right amount of sleep is different for everyone. Some need a solid eight hours while others do well with five hours. You know what amount makes you feel best.

I'm not good at accepting help.

Caregiving cannot be done on your own. It can be hard and tiring. You need emotional support, breaks, advice and encouragement. This only comes from other people. Family, friends, neighbors and strangers want to help you. If you feel alone and lost, support groups, community centers, social workers and religious institutions are great places to start looking for relationships.

Why Don't They do What's Needed?

31

Everyone says something different. It's annoying.

Caregivers have to work with countless different healthcare professionals. Doctors, therapists, hospitals, clinics, home health, etc. It can be very frustrating to tell the same story over and over, get contradictory advice or maybe even be ignored. Caregivers can feel like nobody listens. Keep at it and remember that healthcare professionals do care about your client.

32

Come together and talk it out.

Frustration with healthcare facilities can be difficult to handle. Facilities have a lot of different people doing different things. If all the staff are not on the same page, needed care can get missed. Have care conferences frequently so that everyone can stay on the same page and focus on what's most important to the client, including past history and idiosyncrasies.

33

Remember, you can only change you.

When dealing with frustrating agencies or facilities, remember that the only thing within your control is you. The agency or facility can be encouraged or convinced to provide care the way you want, but they can't be controlled. Take deep breaths, stay calm and politely ask for changes. You'll get a lot more of what you want that way.

34

You believe the words you say.

When working with other healthcare providers who are ignoring things you find very important, please try to avoid over-generalizing. Avoid telling yourself "the doctor is always running late," or "that receptionist is never very helpful." The words you tell yourself are powerful and can add to your frustration. Stick with your specific frustration and be solution-oriented. You'll feel better in the end.

35

You are not a label maker.

When a problem comes up, try to avoid labeling it. Instead, describe it in a sentence or two. It will give you more clarity on what the actual problem is. For example, instead of saying, "The receptionist is rude," which labels the receptionist, describe what was rude, such as "The receptionist didn't give me time, say 'hello' or look at me."

I feel like I need help.

"You" statements can put someone on the defensive right from the get-go. When you use a "you" statement, the person with whom you are trying to solve a problem will get tense and focused on himself. Instead, talk about how you feel. Say something like "I'm frustrated with this care." It starts the conversation with respect, empathy, care and understanding.

Find the blessings in the hardships.

Don't allow frustration to get in the way of positive things. It's easy to forget about the positive when frustration is running high. When you're frustrated, put your situation in a "positive sandwich." State a positive part of care, then state your frustration, and follow up with what you feel is positive again. The provider causing frustration will be more empathetic and willing to solve your problem.

Please stop and talk to me.

Pharmacists are a wealth of information and are great at consultations. But with the emergence of drive-through pharmacies and the hustle and bustle, they tend to quickly read your bottle and go back to work. Ask them questions about interactions (with other meds and foods) and when and how to take meds (with or without food, morning, bedtime, etc.).

Repeating myself over and over and...

Do you get frustrated when taking your client to the doctor's office? You end up telling the receptionist, medical assistant and doctor the exact same information. Before you go to the doctor, write down a list of questions and concerns and also take a current list of meds. Make several copies, then you can just hand them your lists.

Work around the challenges of cyberspace.

If you are doing research on the internet, be sure you are looking at reputable sites. Some good sites include the Centers for Disease Control (cdc.gov) Medscape (medscape.com) or specific agency sites like the American Diabetes Association or The Alzheimer's Association. Going to sites that are not well researched can quickly lead to frustration, anger and wrong information.

When it's Time for the Hospital

Hospitals, stress, confusion and the caregiver

Hospitalizations can be very stressful for the client and the caregiver. They can cause confusion, stress, frustration and anger. Getting through a hospitalization safely and quickly requires team work, collaboration and patience. Caregivers are essential during hospitalization. Caregivers can be a great help to the client in the hospital by being present and ready to answer questions.

Chaos, confusion. One in the same.

According to a Harvard Medical School article in *Harvard Health*, deliriums (sudden and severe confusion) occur in 20 percent of all hospitalized patients, 60 percent of surgical patients and 70 percent of ICU patients. They also note that 40 percent of deliriums can be prevented. Caregivers are essential to this process. Caregivers can provide almost everything needed to prevent or quickly treat a hospital delirium.

Only you know the real truth.

Caregivers and family members can help prevent or recognize a delirium by staying close. Take turns being at the bedside. When the patient wakes up, the caregiver can be a comforting presence. This will help orient the patient. Caregivers also will notice confusion a lot sooner than hospital staff and be able to alert staff to the confusion.

There is no place like home.

Taking a few comforting items to the hospital can ease confusion and familiarize the patient. Pictures of family, friends, or favorite scenes (beaches, forests, city skylines, etc.), and a favorite pillow, blanket, book or music that smell and feel like home, along with a caring caregiver, will ease stress and confusion and minimize the risk of delirium.

"Walking is man's best friend." ~ Hippocrates

Movement is powerful. If possible and safe, get your loved one up and walking a few times a day. If he can't walk, even a simple transfer from bed to the chair will stimulate brain function. The patient who moves around in the hospital will feel better and be able to go home sooner. Just be safe and follow directions.

Be known for the handwritten notes.

A great thing for the caregiver to do while a patient is in the hospital is to take notes. Keep a binder or notebook by the side of the bed and keep track of procedures, labs, medications and notes from the healthcare professionals that come in. Then the caregiver will be better able to answer questions about what happened.

Fail to plan, plan to fail.

Most people who have a chronic illness will need a hospitalization at some time. Plan ahead for this hospitalization. Put together a bag of items needed by the patient, caregiver and hospital staff. Throw in comfort items, a change of clothes, personal effects and important paperwork (power of attorney, advanced directive, insurance cards and medication list).

The truth about the hospital staff.

Hospital staff are very kind and caring people. They are very invested in helping their patients get better. But they are trying to care for a lot of people with scary problems and sometimes the little things get forgotten. Caregivers can be a huge help by giving good personal care, encouraging bed baths and encouraging the patient to eat.

Team means Together Everyone Achieves More!

If your patient lives in a facility, work hard to keep the facility employees informed about what is happening at the hospital. Strongly encourage the discharge planner to call the facility daily to give report. Leaving the facility out will cause a crisis at discharge, especially if they are not prepared to take the patient back.

Ounce of prevention, pound of cure

Hospital acquired infections are a very serious problem. Hand washing for 20 seconds with lots of friction is the number one way to prevent infections from spreading. Caregivers can be a great help by washing their own hands often, encouraging the patient to wash her hands often and reminding the staff to wash their hands thoroughly before touching the patient.

Rub a Dub Dub: Shower Time

51

I really enjoy taking a shower.

Bathing and showering can be so refreshing and comforting. Clean skin, clean hair and a fresh face can do so much for your client's mood and spirit. But bathing and showering can also be stressful and exhausting. A few tricks and tips can make all the difference between tired, angry and frustrated clients and happy, fresh and relaxed clients.

52

Have the courage to display empathy.

A caregiver who is good at bathing has some important personality traits. Empathy is key. Putting yourself in the position of needing someone to bathe you and thinking about how you would feel being naked and vulnerable will really give you some patience. Flexibility to do bathing their way instead of your way will also help increase dignity.

53

How to totally rock their world.

You can totally make your client's day by doing something very easy and very soothing. You see, what most people fear about bathing is being cold. The time right after bathing is the coldest and most uncomfortable. The nicest thing you can do is throw some towels in the dryer before a bath and use warm towels to dry your client off.

Remember, observe dignity in every act.

You can help keep your client's dignity by keeping him covered during bathing. Use a light sheet or a hospital gown. These are easy to clean and easy to dry and your client may feel less vulnerable covered up. Use something that can get wet and that covers loosely so you or the client can wash the body underneath the sheet.

It's not safety first. Safety ALWAYS.

Safety has to be a priority when bathing or showering. The bathroom can be a scary place. When bathing, water goes everywhere. Not just the floor and tub, but condensation gets on all surfaces and makes them slippery to lean on for support. Your durable medical equipment supplier can help you with mats, chairs and other anti-slip products.

It's too hot.
No, too cold.

Make sure that your client or loved one is involved in the temperature of the water. We all have our own preferences of comfortable temperatures. While the water may feel perfectly comfortable and safe to you, your client may find it to be uncomfortably too hot or too cold. Ask your client to check the temperature before bathing starts.

We have to figure out normal.

If your client finds bathing to be stressful, note the time of day when the client is calmest and most cooperative. Also, get to know their normal routines. Some of our elderly people took baths once a week on Saturday night before church the next morning. Some may prefer the evening, before bed. Get to know them.

58

Keep it out of my face!

A lot of elderly people hate having water in their faces. For an elderly client, take extra steps to ensure his face stays dry. Use a handheld shower and let him hold and control it. Allow him to wash his own face, then offer a dry washcloth to hold over his face for the rest of the bath or shower.

59

I have an appointment on Friday.

Women in particular may not want their hair washed. A lot of ladies prefer to go to the salon once a week to have their hair washed and styled. Take extra precautions to keep their hair dry. Use a shower cap. Keep the handheld shower pointed down and rinse their face with a clean, damp washcloth.

A lack of water? No problem.

If it is too hard, too exhausting or not practical to take a bath or a shower, there are a great many rinseless options. Rinseless products do not require water and they do an excellent job of washing and moisturizing. Rinseless washcloths can be heated for comfort. Dry shampoo is a great option to get hair clean.

Up and At 'em: Time to Move

You will feel better after stretching.

Would a weightlifter ever think of lifting something without stretching? Would a marathon runner run 26 miles without loosening up? Nope. They know they would get hurt and not be able to do what they love. Caregivers use their bodies much like athletes do. They lift, bend, stoop and more. Start your day with some good stretching.

On a mission for gait belts.

A transfer belt (also known as a gait belt) is an imperative tool when assisting a client to walk or transfer. The transfer belt is made of a strong material and many have antimicrobial protection. The belt gives you a way to hold onto the person needing assistance securely and comfortably. It's much better than using their clothes.

Use the physical therapists. They're awesome!

Most insurances including Medicare and Medicaid will pay for a physical therapist to come to the home and teach the caregiver how to safely, comfortably and properly move a person with disabilities. Use this opportunity. They can also help get equipment and offer recommendations for the home. Physical therapists are an essential part of the care team.

64

When in doubt, slide, don't lift.

Transfer boards are a great way to assist with transfers, especially if lifting is not possible for the caregiver. A transfer board is a slippery board. One end goes under the buttocks of the client and the other end goes to where the person is transferring (chair, toilet, bed, etc.). The client can slide to where he needs to go.

65

Put your butt to good use.

When transferring a client, never bend at the waist. Instead, bend at the knees and keep the back straight. The back is meant to support you, not lift someone else. It's important to use your strongest muscles during a transfer. When you bend at your knees, you are using your thighs, buttocks and abdomen. This is stronger and safer.

66

Chubby Checkers was wrong. Don't twist.

Another big mistake caregivers make when transferring is not turning their whole body. Twisting at the waist engages the back which, as we've discussed, is not safe or strong. Keep your body straight and turn as a whole. Even when lifting light loads like groceries or bags, turning your whole body will keep your strongest muscles engaged.

They just don't want to fall.

If your client is afraid of falling, transfers will become harder and more dangerous. Clients who are afraid of falling tend to tense up and resist movement. When transferring these clients, caregivers should be patient and in constant communication. Allow the movement to happen in their time and tell them every step of the process.

68

Which side goes first? Goes where?

Always transfer your client to her strong side. If she is going to fall, it will likely happen on her weak side, so engage the strong side for safety. The best way to figure out the strong side versus the weak side is to ask the client. She may be weak due to a stroke or pain from arthritis. When in doubt, choose the side she writes with as the strong side.

Make shoes an investment, not fashion.

With any walking or transferring, always make sure that the client has good, sturdy, non-slip footwear. Slippers are not recommended as they come off the feet too easily. Socks can slip on both hard floor surfaces as well as carpet. Shoes with a closed toe and closed heel are safest. Caregivers should definitely follow this same advice for themselves.

Food: is it Medicine or Poison?

Don't focus on water. Instead, hydration.

Unfortunately, we can be a bit water obsessed and we tend to get angry with folks who don't drink enough. Water is obviously the best choice for a beverage. Its calorie free, increases metabolism and keeps the kidneys healthy. But it's not the only option for hydration. Don't fight or argue with your clients. Hydration is what's most important.

71

Water is not the only option.

If your client despises water and you are ready to give up the water-war, there are other great options to increase hydration and keep clients healthier. Try putting sliced fruit in water to make it sweeter. Decaf tea and coffee are great options. One hundred percent juice given once in a while is good. Just avoid soda and energy drinks.

The more color, the more nutrition.

People are much more likely to eat a nutritious diet if the plate looks pretty. An all brown plate (bread, pasta and corn for example) is not appetizing to the eye. It does not stimulate the appetite. It also tends to be high in calories, but not nutrients. Colorful foods are more appetizing and nutritious.

Stick to the outside. It's better.

Processed foods tend to cause more problems for both stomachs and metabolism. When doing grocery shopping for your client, stick to the outside of the grocery store and avoid going down the aisles. The outside of the grocery store has everything you need, breads, produce, meats and dairy. There are even some goodies there for your client.

A better weight-gain milk shake

Commercial supplements meant to help clients gain and maintain weight are expensive, highly processed and high in sodium. They are an easy and fast way to get calories, but not the best. Instead, try one cup of whole milk, one cup of ice cream and one banana mixed in a blender. You'll get more calories and protein this way.

BRAT refers to diet, not children.

When managing tummy troubles such as nausea or diarrhea, don't reach for the medicine cabinet. Try the BRAT diet. The BRAT diet consists of four foods that are easy on the stomach and effective for treating diarrhea. BRAT stands for Bananas, Rice, Applesauce and Toast. Be sure to see a doctor as well if infection or dehydration are suspected, or symptoms persist.

It's a challenge to be creative.

Don't take away your clients' favorite foods because they have to adhere to a medical diet. Instead, challenge yourself to make their favorite foods according to the diet's requirements. Make healthy substitutions for ingredients that are not so healthy (turkey bacon for breakfast, for example). Also use cooking methods that are healthier (i.e., slow cooker, baking, broiling or grilling).

The fats that are pure evil.

Of all the fats we consume, trans fats are by far the most dangerous and have no health benefit. Trans fats are super sticky and very quickly lead to heart disease, clogged arteries and heart attacks. Read the ingredients, and if any oils are listed as "hydrogenated" or "partially hydrogenated," put it back on the shelf and walk away.

Protein. It does a body good.

Encourage your client to eat a wide variety of proteins. There are many protein sources that don't get the credit they deserve. Beans are high in protein and fiber and low in saturated fat. Lentils are an unsung hero in the protein world. They are yummy and inexpensive. Quinoa is a high protein pasta that is delicious.

Sea salt or table salt. Choose.

Sodium is a silent killer in our foods. Processed foods use sodium as a preservative. Some think that sea salt is better for you than table salt. The truth is that salt is salt and they have the same amount of sodium. Sea salt has a different taste which leads some to eat less of it. In this case, it can be a better alternative.

80

Get back to comfortable, pleasurable meals.

If your client is struggling to adhere to a medical diet, strive to make meals comforting and enjoyable. Focus on what he can eat instead of what he has to give up. Make meals a normal part of the day. Sit down and eat with your client and talk about enjoyable topics. Make meals fun and delicious, not a chore.

Toileting: Number 1 and Number 2

81

When peeing and pooing become hard.

The most common reason that family caregivers decide to put their loved ones in a facility is frustration over toileting. Toileting can be hard and uncomfortable. Take care of yourself, stay calm with accidents and speak openly with your client and doctor about how you feel about toileting. Supportive people will have good options and tricks to help you.

82

Their words are important. Use them.

When assisting someone with toileting, use their words. Everyone talks about the need to toilet in different ways. A proper lady may refer to it as "freshening up" while someone who is crass may talk about "going to the head." Don't become offended by swear words. The language we use is the way we cope with intimate topics.

83

When they just can't make it.

Incontinence is the inability to control urination or defecation. One of the most common causes of incontinence is the inability to get to the bathroom on time. When your client needs to go, it is important to drop whatever you are doing and make getting to the bathroom the most important thing. Don't make your client wait.

Don't be afraid. Get it fixed.

Incontinence can be treated very easily. The majority of people who suffer from incontinence of the bladder are great candidates for treatment. Most don't get treatment because it's embarrassing to talk about. As a caregiver, be sensitive to the issue of incontinence and encourage your client to talk with a doctor about the options.

85

Fluids are important to keep drinking.

The fear of not making it to the bathroom can lead to more serious problems. The most serious being dehydration and urinary tract infections. When people are afraid of incontinence, they stop drinking like they should. Speak kindly and openly with your client about his fears and encourage good hydration. Routine toileting every two or three hours can really help.

Keep trying to find what's right.

Incontinence products are a multi-billion dollar industry. There are so many options. There are products that are worn inside your client's underwear or are worn as underwear. There are products that are disposable or washable. If your client doesn't like using incontinence products, speak with a medical products supplier about alternate options to increase dignity and comfort.

Needing something to hold on to.

Try installing grab bars next to the toilet. Grab bars are fairly inexpensive and can give your client some security and independence. Sometimes just putting up grab bars can make it possible for the client to go on his own. Make sure the bars are properly installed into wall studs as they will have a lot of weight on them.

88

The best caregivers wash their hands.

Don't forget about infection control whenever you are assisting someone with toileting. Gloves must be worn during all aspects of toileting. Hands need to be washed both before and after toileting. The best caregiver will not only wash her own hands, but remember to assist the client in washing his hands as well. It adds normalcy to toileting. It also helps people feel fresher.

89

Pool noodles are not just fun.

If falling is a large concern in the bathroom, consider padding the corners of the counters. Most falls occur in the bathroom, and bathroom falls have the second highest incidence of injury (stairs being the first). An easy way to pad edges is to take pool noodles and slice them down the middle. They will slide right over the edges.

90

Seek help and it will come.

Seek out the services and advice of a good durable medical equipment supplier. There are countless devices that can assist with toileting for both the client and caregiver. Raised toilet seats, bedpans, urinals, bedside commodes, mattress covers incontinence pads, the list goes on and on. A good supplier can work with you to find products to increase safety, dignity and independence.

Six-Word Lessons on Exceptional Caregiving

What Did They Say? I Dunno.

91

Why can't they just hear me?

Communication is so hard in healthcare. Everyone understands the importance of good and open communication, but with such a complicated medical system, healthcare privacy laws and squeamish, weird and uncomfortable ideas about medical issues, communication breaks down constantly. Always strive for patience and openness as you start down the caregiving path. A few prayers wouldn't hurt either.

Keeping everyone involved can be tedious.

Communication chains for family caregivers can be challenging. There are so many people to keep involved. Email will be your hero. You can keep everyone on the same page with the same message. Also check out sites like carepages.com. They allow you to create free blogs where family and friends can check in and offer support.

93

Who do you tell what to?

Facilities like assisted living centers, adult family homes or skilled nursing care can sometimes be a tiny bit confusing to communicate with. Be sure to ask questions and be very clear about who needs what information. Be sure to get it in writing. Do you speak with the administrator, director of nursing, staff nurse, NA-C, etc.?

Put it in a care plan.

The care plan is an essential tool to keep boundaries straight. It puts the client needs into one comprehensive document. All the client's habits, strengths, weaknesses, preferences and needs should be in the care plan. Every little quirk should be added. It's the little things that add to quality of life. This allows for continuity of care.

95

Medicine by a group of physicians

Keeping all the doctors straight and working together can be a feat in and of itself. If your loved one needs several specialists, consider using a group practice for healthcare. A group practice combines primary care doctors together with specialty doctors and therapists. They use the same charts and have agreed-upon protocols for care.

It's a lifeline between two souls.

The key for good communication between the client and the caregiver is more about paying attention to what is not said than what is said. A lot of people, especially the elderly, will not complain or tell you what's wrong. Watch for body language and facial expressions to get a clearer picture of what is in your client's head. Also, watch your own body language and how you communicate.

97

Mind reading's not a college course.

No one knows what you want or need unless you say it. Does your loved one hate having his feet touched? Tell every caregiver who comes near him. Does he need audiobooks? Coordinate the library and the caregivers. Does he need exercises every day? Post a note so everyone can see it--even for the things that seem ridiculous.

I'm sorry; paperwork will get lost.

So much paperwork is needed for so many different roles. Unfortunately, losing critical documents is inevitable, really. Important documents (power of attorneys, living wills, physician orders for life-saving treatments, estate plans, guardianships, etc.) should be scanned to PDF documents and stored on a cloud storage plan. Then when someone loses something, it can easily be shared, emailed or printed, again.

99

Embrace the difficult and the awkward.

The uncomfortable talks are just as important as the comfortable ones. It's vital to encourage your loved one to open up about what she wants done if her heart stops beating or if she becomes unbearably lonely; and her opinions about medications, among other uncomfortable topics. This will bring about trust that goes both ways.

100

There is opportunity for a kindness.

"Please" and "Thank-You" truly will buy you the world. Healthcare professionals are aching and pleading for kindness and politeness. Caregivers who use kindness and humor can get their way 99 percent of the time. They can get moved up in line, get more time with professionals and most importantly, receive some kindness back.

Sources

Vaden, Rory. "Schedule: The Harvest Principle." *Take the Stairs: 7 Steps to Achieving True Success*. New York: Penguin Group, 2012.

Acuff, Jonathan M. "Learning." *Start: Punch Fear in the Face, Escape Average, Do Work That Matters*. Brentwood, TN: Lampo, 2013.

Buffum, Herbert Edward. *The Household Physician, a Twentieth Century Medica; a Practical Description in Plain Language of All the Diseases of Men, Women and Children*. Boston: Physicians' Pub., 1905. Print.

"When Patients Suddenly Become Confused." *When Patients Suddenly Become Confused*. Ed. Anthony Komaroff, M.D. Harvard Health Publications, May 2011. Web. 18 Jan. 2014.

Where I go to get up-to-date Information

CDC.gov – Centers for Disease Control. The go-to source for peer reviewed, reliable information on everything; chronic illnesses, infectious disease; smoking cessation and so much more

Medscape.com – the latest research on illness, medications, treatments, healthcare and professionalism

Diabetes.org - American Diabetes Association

Alz.org - Alzheimer's Association

CarePages.com – To create blogs and invite friends and family to check in on the things going on in your loved one's life. Great for keeping other family members involved, especially if they are living far away.

See the entire Six-Word Lesson Series at *6wordlessons.com*

www.ingramcontent.com/pod-product-compliance
Lightning Source LLC
Chambersburg PA
CBHW062008070426
42451CB00008BA/292